101

REASONS

PEOPLE

GET

FIRED

BEN. E. ODJES

FOR STELLA AND OLIVIA

CONTENTS

INTRODUCTION

This small but mighty book was written to equip you with the right information you need to excel in the corporate arena and escape the most dreaded nightmare of every employee the world over- Getting Fired.

This book was inspired by my father who worked so hard in a federal organization, making sure he put in extra hours and sweated more than his colleagues only to wake up one day to find the lay-off letter waiting at his desk.

It takes more than hard work! And there are thousands of employees who experience the same everyday.

To escape this evil, this book contains practical guidelines and hard truths that can see you through. You won't find a hundred and one reasons here, but the core reasons that leads getting fired are well researched and treated to guide you through.

CHAPTER ONE

HIGH ABSENTEEISM RATE

No employer wants to keep an employee who keeps bolting in and out of the work environment and making millions of excuses.

One of the top ten reasons why people get fired is absenteeism. No employer wants to keep a staff or employee who keeps bolting out of the work environment and making millions of excuses. No matter how genuine your excuses may be, it negatively affects productivity when you absent your self from your place of work.

Managements have different response to this, as some management would not tolerate an absentee rate of five (5). That is when you stayed away from the job just five days in a year. This brings in the sack letter as ordained by the principles guiding the management but unknown to most employees. Worse still, some will not allow an AR of 2 or even 1!

Whenever you absent yourself from work, a link in the chain of work gets broken and normal functioning of the mechanism is arrested or slowed down. Even when you think someone else, maybe a close colleague, could help out, it is never the same. His stress capacity is affected and he ends up doing the job slowly. Also, doing so with relatively more errors. All these are retrogressive towards achieving the business organization's goals and objective. Productivity and efficiency is retarded. And this is what your boss hate to discover.

There are even cases whereby absenteeism had led to severe injuries or death to the 'unspecialized' worker. Because he or she is not that specialized in that particular area, he or she commits lethal errors and the shocking consequences follow.

Now what do you think the management would do to the 'missing' employee after such an ugly incident had taken place?

Fire him of course!

CHAPTER TWO

LOW PRODUCTIVITY

THE PRODUCTIVE EMPLOYEE CLIMBS UP THE
LADDER WHILE OTHERS ARE STILL TRYING
TO GET ON THEIR FEET.

One strong reason people get fired is low productivity. Your performance at the job is what you would be judged by. Performance appraisal measures your productivity and lets your boss or the management know how well you are doing. And vice versa. If your productivity is found to be lagging behind repeatedly, then your name gets written in the black book. And in no time or sometimes spontaneously, you get kicked out. Just like that. But it is clear the un-productive employee dug his or her career grave with his or her own hands over the years. He or she kept doing so each passing day by being less productive than their colleagues. This makes you the weak link in the corporate chain and exposes you to the mercy of your employer.

To be productive is what the stakeholders want. In the banking [marketing] world a set target is often given to employees. Once an employee fails to meet the target over and over again, his usefulness to the bank gets stabbed right in the heart. Same goes for every other business organization; from production factories to services. Employee's share of work is often dished out sometimes in groups. Now this is where most employees get it all wrong. Most like to disappear in the crowd when given a group task. They dissolve away like salt in water and allow the smart people to show how smart they are; how productive they are. How creative they are, and how much leadership potential they carry on the inside. But little do they know or remember that group work is often a test. One with which certain kind of appraisal is carried out. And there they are losing out their opportunities. A damn good opportunity to show their bosses what they are made of, what they are capable of.

On the contrary when an employee is productive he is hardly underestimated or underrated. He become the boss's choice person when its time to delegate duties or authority. This quality gives your boss peace of mind and he would rather leave the job to you. Don't get me wrong, not his job, but your job, or the group task. The productive employee climbs up the ladder when others are still trying to get to their feet. And soon, he becomes his former colleagues' boss. Why? Because hard work pays. He obviously gets his reward from putting a little extra input than the others. In so doing he is helping the organization get to the finish line of the set goals and objectives a little faster. On the contrary, the less productive employee is regarded as relatively doing the opposite.

Low productive level in the office is often associated to employees conducting personal business in the office, talking or chatting too much with other employees and wasting precious time that could have been invested in doing meaningful tasks.

Often times the unproductive employee is found on the internet, conducting his or her own business sending emails, browsing sex-content websites, engaging in social networking activities or worse still, on the phone talking to friends. These are all counter- productive. And once a habit is formed on these set-backs it becomes an everyday affair and your productivity level drops to the bottom dead centre. And the best the organization could do is to have you FIRED!.

Therefore to keep your priceless job instead of losing it, try to concentrate on the job. Think of results and performance and how to outdo your colleagues.

CHAPTER THREE

DOCTORED RESUME

OF ALL THE CRAFTS TO BE AN HONEST MAN
IS THE MASTER CRAFT.

Extensively, more and more organizations are painstakingly taking their time out to check up and confirm whatever their staff resume says about them. From city to city across the globe organization seem to be at the brink of employees who doctored their resume [s] just to give them the opportunity to be employed.

This is so because over the years many crappy resume[s] have been doctored, given a super facelift, such that warrant an express employment, only for the employer to discover that the employee(s) is performing below expectation. This calls for suspicion and the employee gets investigated, an attempt to know his true academic background. And over the years growing numbers of doctored resume(s) have been discovered, and therefore it ought to be checked, otherwise many half baked 'experts' or 'professionals' would find themselves in offices they hardly merited.

Tending a doctored resume before your employer is a crime on its own and against the regulations of the organization. So once discovered, the management may decide to get you FIRED!

Don't lie about your resume. Let the information be true. Let it remain so. Let it promise less, that is, if it were so, and you give more to your organization, in terms of performance.

If you've already done that, you may take a bold step by reporting yourself to the management and try talking things out. That honest act may make a right thinking boss to forgive, and retain you. But the case is however different when they get to discover themselves.

Lying on a resume simply tells the organization you are not a honest person. It tells them your integrity is questionable. And no boss wants to keep a staff like that.

CHAPTER FOUR

DISHONEST PRACTICES

"MAN'S DARKEST HOUR IS WHEN HE SITS DOWN TO PLAN HOW TO GET MONEY WITHOUT EARNING IT" HORACE GREELEY

Trust is the force that turns the wheels of business. Without trust nobody would put in millions of dollars into a 'stranger's' hands or bank account and expect the desired service or product to be rendered or delivered. Trust is the hard brick on which businesses are built. Trust is essential to business.

Your boss expects this essential quality from you. Dishonesty and fraud kills this quality. And once dead, its resurrection is almost impossible in the corporate arena.

Accountability is required of you. It is one of your challenges especially when you work in a bank or you are a PR person or the accountant of your organization.

If your boss gives you a thousand dollars to run a project, and then you found out it takes five hundred bucks to accomplish it, don't be stupid about it. Return the rest to him. Why? Because he is not stupid! He has been there; done that, a thousand times before you might even have tried it at all. Get the picture quite clear now?

A lot of temptation creeps into the mind once you are in the office that deals with money. Dishonest practices revolve around this sphere. And it has cost a lot of people their job. You may think you are smart about it. But guess what? They will get you soon.

I know a smart-ass banker who succeeded in fooling the bank for four whole years. Now that's a real smart ass. In a short while after being employed he has got himself properties everywhere. But just one fateful day got him to lose all the properties, lose his job, and got thrown behind bars! He got nailed for fraud.

You sure don't want to end up like him. So learn to be honest and trustworthy. It will make you climb up the corporate ladder faster than you think, and make you keep your job instead of losing it.

The corporate environment is really like a battle arena. People are bent to do whatever to climb up, even if it means stepping over anybody. This is hard truth, and the real deal.

Colleagues compete with each other daily, though not often visible. Or I should say noticeable. Corrupt or dishonest practices may just be the hard evidence your colleague may use against you. And once you are exposed, you are off the job.

CHAPTER FIVE

DRUG AND ALCHOHOL ABUSE

DRUG ABUSE IS A TIME BOMB, A SUICIDE
MISSION TO EMPLOYEE'S JOB

One common cause of job loss is drug and alcohol abuse. Drug abuse is climbing up the ladder in every major city in the world. Both drug and alcohol abuse has harmful effect on the human system and a negative effect on our performance at the job.

Contrary to popular belief alcohol destroy more lives than hard drug use. This is because alcohol has more 'fans' than hard drugs. Alcohol is readily available over the counter and most people seem to run to it when they think they are stressed or faced by a nagging problem. Even a nagging wife make many men rush into the arms of alcohol.

Alcohol is a gentle killer, because its effect is slow yet eventually destructive. Imagine a factory worker addicted to alcohol? He is going to be faced by continual inconsistency, unreliable performance and an unwelcome behaviour in the corporate arena.

This unwelcome inconsistency will continually make the boss or foreman frown at his work and behaviour and pour out an avalanche of queries on him. And eventually have him FIRED.

Alcohol is readily abused by most people than hard drugs which are relatively scarce around most homes. Several thousands of people have lost their jobs around the world due to drugs and alcohol abuse.

The best way to escape this kind of problem is to abstain from alcohol if you can. But if you can't, moderation, especially when you are back from work should be what you should work on. Taking alcohol on the job or before going to your place of work should be totally discontinued and discouraged. This way you may have overcome or escaped a time bomb which would've exploded all around you and send you into the labour market. And not only that, endanger your family with a total cut off of income supply.

CHAPTER SIX

DO YOU LOVE YOUR JOB?

A MAN'S HEART IS WHEREVER HIS TREASURE IS.

Be sincere, what is your answer to that question? Yes or No? Well, in reality, the truth is many people don't love their job. How could you? It makes you jump start the day, waking up by 4 or 5am in the morning to prepare for work. You wanted to be on the bed at that particular time and continue your great good sleep. But there goes the alarm! And you grumble out of bed, because you NEED to.

This psychologically program most people not to love their job. They are just doing it as a matter of necessity, you know, no work, no pay. So they need to go to work just to make ends meet not because they really love it. Don't get me wrong, some people *do* love their job. Those doing what they truly love and getting fat pay- check for it.

But if this is not right, that is if you don't love the kind of job you are doing now, then everything will finally go bad. It's like a system. Everything is either directly or indirectly connected to each other. The burning desire to get work early on your own wont be there. Then you are hardly punctual. Again the zeal to put in your best in every situation or occasion is hardly there, and that makes you lukewarm at your job. Your boss starts seeing the loose ends, your nonchalant attitude on the job. And even right then, he writes you off even though the lay of letter is yet to arrive.

The solution is- Fake it, until it becomes Real, yes, you just have to keep 'faking' to love your job until it actually becomes a part of you. Psychologist found out a long time ago that what we do repeatedly and consistently for about twenty one days, at least, becomes a part of us.

But come to think of it, if you really consider it all you will realize that your job plays a very important role in your life. It pays the bills. At least right now, so it is important that you take it seriously and *love* it for that until you could find may be a better one.

CHAPTER SEVEN

NOT FOLLOWING INSTRUCTIONS.

"THE UNWISE DESPISE WISDOM AND INSTRUCTION" PROV 1-7

Before engaging in writing this book, as with every other good book, I did a great deal of research into the matter- why do people get fired, and believe me you, I got a hundred and one reason. Some are so incredible, but they actually got someone fired, no, they actually got thousands of employees fired.

Among the reasons, one of the top five reasons is Not Following Instructions, a smoky job-killer!

Insubordination is the worst thing an employee could do at his or her place of work. It will bring in the layoff letter fast. And not only that, most people hear people talk and generalize on the opinions or ideas, instead of listening carefully and intelligently underline the main words. For example, your boss wants you to take up a parcel and hand it over to a courier service, say KHL or there about. You listened to him in a rush and rush up with the parcel down the street in the hot afternoon sun, and KHL is about a thousand feet away. And you threw a glance at your side, and there you go MHL. *"Oh stupid, why go down the street. When the bottom line is getting the parcel mailed to Mr. Tom? I'll patronize MHL instead and save my self the hassle and get back to my job at the office."* And that's exactly what you did. Then you went back, the workaholic boss is gone for an appointment. Two days later he got a complaint and summons you to his office.

"Why didn't you mail the parcel to Mr. Tom on time?"

"I did."

"But he didn't get it on time?"

"I swear to God, I mailed it even earlier than you expected".

"How do you mean?"

"I did what you asked under five minutes the moment you asked me to. I gave it to MHL."

"Holy shit, that snail speed mailing failure! You have made us to loose a five million dollar contract, you idiot. I said mail it through KHL!"

Now your legs begin to wobble and its like you are peeing in your pants. And then you apologize…..

"I 'm ….. I'm sorry".

Then he looks at you straight in the eyes and says…..

"You are fired!"

Every employee who wants to keep his or her job should be very particular with instructions. Every instruction from your boss carries a hidden reason. If you cannot grasp that reason, then you will badly interpret the message and end up doing the wrong thing. You may even put in your best trying to ensure that you satisfy him, but to your surprise it turns out damn real bad.

You can ask your boss the question again, paraphrasing the sentence he had said if you don't clearly get it in the first place. And automatically he would paraphrase the instructions again, a strong passion inside burning, this time to push it across to you clearly, vivid and unambiguous. In so doing you will save yourself a lot of troubles in the future. You will avoid rebukes, queries, anger, grudge, dislike and hate. All which could lead to getting you thrown out into the labour market.

Again, if you were given a set of instructions by your boss and you 'strongly' know that it would bring in negative results, don't try to correct him or go on and do your own thing. Be like a solider, obey order before complaining. But you may go around and tell him what you fear might be the consequence in camera. He may just realize his mistake or clarify the intricacies that you aren't aware of and save you the odds.

CHAPTER EIGHT

NOT KNOWING YOUR LIMIT

"A GOOD GENERAL NOT ONLY SEES THE WAY TO VICTORY; HE ALSO KNOWS WHEN VICTORY IS IMPOSSIBLE" POLYBIUS

There is a limit to the amount of 'corporate freedom' that is allowed every employee. And beyond that limit you are viewed as poking your nose into another man's privacy. This is serious, and really not a joke.

Do you know your limit?

Your boss may want you around sometimes and want you off his territory in next moment. He or she may choose to, by reason of allowing for proper free flow of up down or down up/ formal or informal communication, become more friendly than he or she is supposed to.

And this is where most people dig their graves. Why? Because many people start taking his or her closeness for granted and find themselves challenging orders and challenging authority without even knowing it. And when you start doing that, you think well, its Joe anyway, he's a friend, I can tell him the truth or what's right in this situation. Of course you can tell him or her truth, but never let it be close to disobeying him or challenging orders. That amounts to challenging authority.

Once the boss notices this, he cuts you off his free flow communication link, blacking you out. And automatically starts looking for holes in your job with which to nail you to the cross. Then all the little mistakes he has been ignoring start becoming unforgivable blunders.

The only way not to fall into this trap is to know your limit and not poke your nose about into your boss's affair. This doesn't necessarily mean you shouldn't be aware of whatever is going on but don't be stupid about it.

Got it? Or it may cost you your job

CHAPTER NINE

POOR HEALTH CONDITION

HEALTH IS WEALTH

Health is wealth, is a popular saying that cannot be over emphasized especially in words but when it comes to 'doing' time, most people underestimate the wisdom in those words, taking them for granted, boozing and cascading avalanche of alcohol and cigarettes for example, down into their system. The fact that these time-bombs do not immediately explode in their system somehow seems to fool them into believing they have no negative effect in their lives.

I knew a popular broadcaster who messed up his kidneys because of too much booze and cigarette. His lifestyle is the carefree type. He thinks he's got a good job and good paycheck. So he could just go on and 'enjoy' his life. Friends and family have repeatedly talked to him about this 'bad habit' but certainly to no avail. The result?

Bang!

He messed up his kidneys! And had other complications related to heavy smoking. The broadcast house was merciful enough not to worsen his condition, but to help him out. So they kick up a foundation, a foundation in his name and ended up raising a huge amount of money to enable the kidney donation and transplant to take place. And it all went well. The transplant was successful, and he still kept the job. Lucky him, I would say.

Years later. A few years later. The condition came back! How? And why? Well, he went back to the same health killing life. And now, nobody deeply felt sorry for him. It became difficult, and sounded stupid to raise money from the people again to solve a problem they thought they had already solved, if not for the man's foolishness.

It became imperative to let go. The organization has a limit; it could not continue to suffer at the mercies of anybody. It has to continue living and not just that but profitably, if not the stakeholders will all be at the mercies of the dying man's loses. He ended up dead; lost his job and life.

When I was growing up as a boy, I remember my mum has a particular condition akin to diabetes yet they always say it isn't exactly diabetes.

It got her several visits and admission at the company hospital. It was like a day in day out thing. And my dad had to keep making excuses and taking permission to go and care for her at the hospital.

It was so bad that she was actually confirmed dead once, and we had to break the news to the rest of the family and started making burial arrangement. Then miraculously after several long hours, she got up on her own.

But here is where I am going. The tonnes of excuses bothered his boss a lot and it became imperative for him to do something about it. He started booking my dad absent each time he asked for permission to go care for my sick mother.

The result?

He got early retirement and was psychologically broken down. It came at a time he was waiting for a promotion that would have changed our life. He got literally fired for being there for her.

Several years later, I found myself ransacking some prescriptions papers and discovered my mum on her own part didn't strictly adhere to the doctor's prescription. Health is wealth; keep your health keep your job.

CHAPTER TEN

BRINGING 'HOME PROBLEMS' TO THE OFFICE

LET SLEEPING DOGS LIE

Have you seen the movie - *I think I love my wife*? Well, if you have, you now have a two way path to understanding this problem, by the time you are through with this vital part of this great good book. Man is a social animal that lives in a social system of one kind or another. We have relatives and relations. Family and friends. Neighbours and acquaintances. All these connect to us one way or another and exhibit certain influence in our lives. According to studies, a man's immediate family is the one with the strongest hold on the man's concern. He worries for their safety, health, clothing, food and shelter just the way he worries over these for himself. And in several times, he is more concerned about them more than himself.

Basically, the state of a man's immediate family determines his own state of happiness, productivity and effectiveness. A man suffering from the mortal blows of unhappy marriage naturally carries the disappointments, anger and the need to blame someone to the office. Once in the office he becomes clumsy as the job suddenly become cumbersome and displeasing. All he needs is a soothing balm, that magical recipe that can heal his heart and save it from the nervous breakdown, but there is a kilogram of paperwork, or a two tonne machine with about two dozen buttons or switches to operate, right in front of him !

Will he put in his best shot?

Absolutely, he would end up putting in his best shots of confusion. And every little mistake he makes may end up causing the organization loses worth real good millions. Yes, every little one translates to loses that the boss won't take lightly because you are either directly or directly putting hot coals beneath his feet. And his response? Come on, you know this already- BAD!

In the aforementioned movie, the victim's lack of love, sex and romance in his marriage ended him up trapped in the love nest of an old friend and it became difficult for him to concentrate on his job. Soon he starts putting pleasure before business. He secretly leaves the office to steal moments with the new tadpole in town. He misses appointments, vital appointments, causing his boss to yell and scream. And the organization loosing its face before their clients. And that means losing millions. Big money!

In return he got queries and hot threats, his job hanging on the line. A little push and he is cast down into the 'fired- people' Hell, the simmering heat already scorching him.

There are those whose whole condition may not have involved another   woman or man, as the case may be, from the outside, you know, outside the family, but the case is still the same. The result remains the same. You get knocked off the right track.

You hardly concentrate anymore on you job. It suddenly makes no sense to you. It becomes rubbish and you don't want to hear the truth that your well wishers at your place of work are telling you. Something like 'boy, you're loosing it'. So you go on and get it all deeply messed up and that is misconduct, all bad for your career or job in every way. So what do you do?

Well, the best way to solve this kind of problem is not bringing it into your place of work in the first place. You also need to talk things out yourself. And if you wouldn't see a marriage counselor as fast as you could, you are only helping to clear the small path into a road for the beast to come into the village. You are only trying to complicate things and get FIRED

CHAPTER ELEVEN

DISLOYALTY

LOYALTY IS A MEAL EMPLOYERS CRAVE FOR.

How loyal are you to your boss? How loyal are you to your colleagues? How loyal are you to your organization?

In every organizational setting loyalty plays a vital role. A very very important part to your career's future. It could either make it bright or bleak, depending on what you choose to do with it. It could either make you, or break you.

It is imperative for employees to be loyal to their employer. It is an essentially quality that your boss demands of you. You are expected to be faithful and loyal and not the other way round.

A disloyal employee would never be a committed one. He is hardly supportive, and will turn his back against his boss in trouble times. Such a person or staff will, once the boss get himself back together again, face his wrath. And this wrath will only make the stupid, disloyal staff to further the frontiers of his disloyal attitude and earn him rebukes, queries, suspension or get him fired.

Loyalty is a meal that employers crave for. Your boss craves your loyalty, and once he can't find it in you, he regrets having you around. He finds you untrustworthy with certain vital information. Therefore he restricts you, limiting you every way he can. He edits a lot of beneficial information and throws the scrap part at your desk. And because you are working with very limited information or you have only a superficial idea about the entire nature of the job you are supposed to do, you would end up having it done poorly. And then you get blasted for that again. You get queries. Got it? But once you are loyal, he notices it, and welcomes you with open arms. Your presence strikes the right cords inside of him. He is happy with you and feels confident, secure and more capable getting things. When it is necessary to delegate any special job, he shoves it your way. And   because you are loyal you would do it in such a way that he ponders "I couldn't have done it any better!".

And this creates the opportunity for you to get more of that. And more and more.

This is leverage.

This is what makes you stand out among your colleague. And when its time for promotion, you stand out among them too.

Now that's the boss.

How about your loyalty to your colleagues? Does it count?

Once you are loyal or disloyal to your colleague you reap the good or bad fruit you've sown. Garbage in, garbage out. You get what you asked for.

Being disloyal to your colleagues will make them sideline you. They mount a big psychological wall between you and them. It gets so strong yet invisible but the effect can be perceived. They make you an island. An island surrounded by desert instead of water. There is a corporate 'anointing' that you are supposed to benefit from.

But you don't get to find it around. This renders you of very little use and de-values you. You start messing up things and even when you make a little mistake they react as if you've made a grave mistake. Your boss treats you likewise because it's a corporate chain- reaction. If they could not trust you why should he?

Got it?

CHAPTER TWELVE

LUKEWARM ATTITUDES

YOUR GLORIOUS CERTIFICATE CAN GET YOU
THE JOB BUT IT REALLY CANT KEEP IT.

Job Security is the biggest challenge of modern day workers. With the high rate of unemployment, nobody wants to get thrown out into that economic dungeon. Therefore the fear is vivid, alive and boisterous in our hearts.

Competition rocks business environments like a raging storm. This demands a whole lot from CEOs/ MDs and the rest of the heads and stakeholders of any meaningful organization. Therefore, more and more is expected of employees. And any one who could not cope with the speed gets left behind. Or maybe that's just a calmer way of putting it – gets FIRED maybe more appropriate.

Your 'glorious' certificate can get you the job, but it really can't keep it. What can keep you the job surely isn't your certificate. Yes, indeed. It is your performance!

No employer prefers to keep a lukewarm employee under his payroll. And even when they do and tolerate such employee(s) these still turn out to be the first to get the dismissal letter once the economic weather or climate of the organization turns out to be unfavorable.

You know why?

Well, I'll tell you. People need to put the blame of every unfavorable thing, event, experience or result on something or someone. And in this case it turns out the management just have to flip through their records and BANG! There you are – that lukewarm bastard! Hard truth. I really needn't soften it.

Vibrancy in your job circle makes you a person after the heart of the business. Such persons hardly have blames directed at them in their places of work and even if they make a mistake most people hardly see it. They just ignore it like it was nothing.

God himself doesn't like Lukewarmness as the bible said 'because you are lukewarm, and not burning, I will spew you out'.

How much more imperfect man? Being Lukewarm in your place of work makes you appear less meaningful to the organization and therefore likely dispensable. With this aura hanging over the lukewarm employee, he or she suddenly becomes dispensable when the need to fired one or two staff arises. Now let's not fool ourselves – that need comes. It necessarily comes in reality, especially when the economic climate isn't favorable anymore.

Many multinationals that you think offer such great job security still experience this too. There is a multinational that had to call it off, at least a big part of their operations in a country in West Africa, and fired thousands, retaining a few while it relocates to another country, after operating in that country for decades, about fifty years! You see, it happens everywhere and you don't have to sit on your butt in that lazy office chair and think all is well just because your pay check is still coming when you know deep down inside that you suffer from this condition? Or it is actually your organization that is suffering from your condition.

You've got to wake up from that slumber land before you find yourself in a nightmare. You need to dust your ass and get vibrant. Every organization demand vibrancy from its staff and not lukewarmness. Though being lukewarm does not mean you aren't working. No, but it means you are not working that much. It means you parade yourself as a dispensable piece of shit. It means you are sitting on a time bomb. And when the right time comes, it's going to explode and throw you into the labour market.

Now do a brief appraisal of yourself. Are you vibrant or lukewarm?

I learned about the negative and destructive power of being lukewarm on your job a long time ago. It was a painful experience that finds it hard to leave my mind. I remember it a lot when I see lukewarm people snailing about in their place of work. And I pity them a lot because I know where they are headed.

Several years back I became the acting senior prefect in my secondary school. I went about doing my job. I was inexperienced anyway, and I could also say, was plagued by a handful of the negative conditions you will find in this book.

I was lukewarm. I wasn't burning at all. Well, but thanks, at least I accepted the truth. I was doing the job but not burning on the job. I had in my workforce a vibrant Assembly Prefect He was really burning and I could see it. I thought I was getting the glory from the school authority, I witnessed a reshuffling that kicked me to the laboratory and Joseph, the Assembly Prefect, made the senior prefect instead. This happen everyday, everywhere. In diverse places of work. And there's no other way to escape it other than a truthful self appraisal. Ask yourself if you really think you are vibrant on the job or portray a lukewarm attitude towards it. Jesus said, and you shall know the truth and it shall set you free.

Now if you are not vibrant on the job please accept the truth that you are sleeping on it. You are sleeping on a part of your future. An important one that can affect you and your family either negatively or positively.

CHAPTER THIRTEEN

PUNCTUALITY

PUNCTUALITY IS THE SOUL OF BUSINESS

The opening quote is a very popular one that everybody knows so well. But come to think about it, despite this fact many people (employees) still find it really tasking to keep up with time. And everyday they are so ready, so eager, to tender their reasons before their bosses and think all that actually solves anything. Does it really do that? We shall find out.

City life is not really a bed of roses. I know someone who wakes up 4am in the morning to prepare for work everyday. And comes back home at 10pm. 'That is crazy', I can hear someone saying. But that is how demanding some employment can be. He had to 'travel' from one end of the state to another everyday, to make a living. And why does he wake up that early? Well, I guess you know already – Traffic. The last time we met he was saying something like – leaving the job for good. Then I asked why. And he told me either regular lateness or the stress was still eventually going to knock him out of the job, directly or indirectly. I nodded understandingly and told him "that is true"

Same goes for everyone that is in the same shoe today. Funny enough, there are many people who don't have to travel long distance like my friend, Peter, but surprisingly they have a late–coming record at their place of work. They are perpetual latecomers. This is surely no good at all. It dents your personal corporate image and may and will get this kind of people fired sooner than they think.

So if you want to escape this fire make certain punctuality at your place of work is taken as serious business.

CHAPTER FOURTEEN

UNSOCIABLE ATTITUDES

NO MAN IS AN ISLAND

Being unsociable, in your place of work is like making yourself *a nun in a 'Pro' house.* Definitely, and most definitely there is a perceivable strong voice in the air that says – *you are not welcome here.*

Man is a social animal. Simply put he mixes. However not everybody is actually 'social'. Some people live in their own inner shell. They naturally want to be left alone to themselves. They want to avoid people and expect people to avoid them. Yes, that's true. Even in their place of work they still share the same view and it shows in the manner of way they behave towards others. This can be very confusing. It can cause co-workers to build the wrong view about oneself. And trust me, that view or opinion will surely be negative. It may make one appear to be unreachable. It may limit the extent to which positive opinions and ideas can be shared between co-workers and therefore lead to inefficiency. The active personnel manager will spot this big gap. And this gap is what he hopes to bridge to encourage job efficiency. Now the personal that unconsciously continue to commit this offense is in for trouble – queries.

Unsociable attitudes will, simply put, make your co-workers dislike you. And once you are disliked by many in your place of work, you are already a leg out of the door. Why? Because people will continually complain about you, criticize you, tempt you, set you up, and pray to bring you down so they could laugh at you. And these all happens under the corporate roof. Yes it does!

Being unsocial is a psychological thing. It is a condition that mostly drags in from childhood to adulthood when unnoticed and unchecked. It is a time bomb. And it explodes in your face every day in every organization.

Sorry enough, the sufferer mostly never realizes his or her problem. He doesn't see it. He doesn't even know it exist. He is blind to it. And that's why he or she ends up being ravaged by it.

The work environment is a social network of a different setting. A corporate social network. A social system. And that means everything connects and relates to each other one way or the other. Everything is interdependent. And no man is an island. Therefore the unsocial employee seems to be the weak link in the system and when the time for appraisal comes he or she is spotted out and will get the blows. And several of those blows will eventually turn into a corporate TKO. And then the enemy within the unsocial employee gets him fired. You see the link? God!

Now what if you are this type?

What do you do?

How do you help yourself?

Well, you have to start by deciding to be friendlier right away without wasting time. You have to kick that door open. You've got to open your hands and welcome whoever cares to come close in the corporate scene. In the beginning you may notice you don't appear to be real. Why? Because it is a different you and it is only natural that you start feeling fake. Well, I guess you just have to continue 'faking' it until it becomes real. And to tell you the truth, you will end up becoming it, because after a few weeks it would have become a habit. And by then you will find it so easily to mix up and share your thought, views, opinions, ideas etc positively in line with the organizations' goals and objectives. This way you are doing yourself and your organization as a whole lot of good.

CHAPTER FIFTEEN

POOR CREATIVITY

CREATIVITY IS THE SOUL OF ADVANCEMENT.

Every employer wants a creative employee to work with. Every employer needs people who can make positive contributions to the overall goals and objectives of the organization. But unfortunately, only few people are really creative yet everyone carries the creative ability in them!

A creative employee gains the favour of the employer. This puts him or her in the 'special people group (SPG) exists in every organization. Yes it does, though you won't find it written anywhere in the block of offices or in the bulletins, releases etc.

Creativity plays a vital role both to your career excellence and job security. A creative person says, by his or her action – 'look here folk, I am loaded. I can handle it.' But an uncreative person by his or her action tells the management and colleagues – I am helpless in this situation. And remember – action speaks louder than words.

Now tell me if you were the manager and you are faced by challenges that call for trimming down workforce, which of the two described above will you retain or fire?

You got it.

Some managers won't even wait till then! Reactive managers may not give employees that are not creative a chance. They would want to have him or her fired immediately and bring in fresh blood. That is the very nature of it.

To be creative one has to open his mind to a number of other suggestions, ideas, notions, thoughts, hunches etc, especially when the normal methods of going about solving the problem isn't bringing any positive result. Once the suggestions and ideas are in place, then one has to sort them out to see which one would be feasible and viable. This can be hard job to the very – uncreative personality at first, but, with a little practice –

freeing your inner mind to do the 'thinking' instead of prejudicing it with your own views it becomes easier everyday. There are a million ways to having anything done. We simply stick to the popular once. Don't limit yourself with your 'thinking'.

And more important you have to know when you apply creativity, when it is expected of you. You just don't 'freestyle' on the methods of operations given to you by the organization. No! That is wrong. You only have to pull up strength from your creative reservoir when the normal method suddenly seems to be ineffective in achieving the result. And you don't have to do it all by yourself. You could go to your boss and make your suggestion. And once it is effective, bang! Then let him take the glory. And you get that? Okay, I'll say it again – LET HIM TAKE THE GLORY, that is if its possible and you'd be favored for that later.

CHAPTER SIXTEEN

STAGNANCY

FLOW LIKE A RIVER AND YOU WILL GET TO THE OCEAN

It is wrong to remain in the same position over the years. You came into the arena as a clerk and remain the same for a decade with no additional value that you can boast of. Then you are simply celebrating mediocrity and limiting your career's potential.

There is no crime in starting small, but remaining thesame over the years is what is actually bad. People who are stagnant in their place of work only remain there out of pity. Yes, their bosses just let them be instead of having them fired or demoted. These are people that should really be promoted not otherwise. But because they don't know that either by qualification or performance they are stagnant they would remain so until their bosses one day chooses to let go of sentiments and focus on efficiency and targeted goals and objectives. And then they fired.

My father once told me a story about his life working as a civil servant. He had remain in the same position for twelve years! Yes, that is actual true. Until one day his boss called him to his office and sat him down right in front of him.

"I want to promote you, but I don't have enough strong reasons to prove you earn it. You've had opportunities to go for several courses and better your qualification but you've never considered it. I advise you to do that right away."

"But I've worked hard ever since!"

"Yes, and so have a few of your colleagues. You've got to distinguish yourself from the others." Guess what he did? He went back to school part-time and got the promotion he had been laboring hard for a whole twelve years in two years!

CHAPTER SEVENTEEN

HOW DEDICATED ARE YOU?

"THE WORLD HAS LITTLE NEED FOR THE
WEAK AND FAINTHEARTED"

-MARDEN

Are you dedicated to your job? Do a quick self appraisal and give yourself a truthful answer. Now what makes you think your boss and other colleagues don't see it. If you are dedicated to your job it will show. You can't hide it. But if you are not, well think again.

The management and stakeholders want a dedicated staff on their pay roll. The dedicated employee goes the extra mile rendering priceless service to the organization. These are the kind of people even you would want to work for you. Isn't that true?

Once you are dedicated it shows in everything you do. Every part you play in the production process. To be dedicated is to be ready to sacrifice other needs to render quality service to your organization. That is, putting your job first before other things. An employee who is dedicated gets noticed.

His or her action speaks louder than words. It speaks for itself and he needn't go about shouting it for every body to hear.

A dedicated employee retains his job, and an undedicated one will no sooner end up loosing it and find himself in the labour market.

Once you are not dedicated it reflects in all that you do. There is a glaring nonchalant attitude in the way you carry out your job. There is a clear, vivid and smoky inefficiency in all you do. Your part is always badly played and that means you are performing at low ebb when you are expected to be on top of it.

Dedication is commitment. You have to be committed. It is the willingness to work hard and give your energy and time to your job. Any employee who is dedicated, committed to his or her job will hardly get kicked out. Only a crazy idiot, a stupid boss will do that. Or tell me would you want to fire a hard working employee if you need to down size your workforce when the need arise? Absolutely no! Rather you would fire the employee that is nonchalant with his job. Because if you fire the dedicated ones you would only be doing your organization more harm. And a sensible boss would never do that.

It takes a lot to be committed. It is a quality sacrificial service it is distinguished service, one that is noticeable by the rest of your colleagues and your boss. It takes your time and energy. A lot of them both, more than normal, yes, and that is what makes it unique. And that uniqueness is what makes you also, a unique employee. And your efforts gets spotted, and waiting to be rewarded.

Once you are not dedicated to your job you consciously or unconsciously neglect a lot of things. You don't see a lot of holes to fill. You are half blind to many little responsibilities. And worse of all you would rationalize and sum it all up- *well, these scarcely matters*. But tell you what, they do.

Why? Because it is these 'little things' that adds up and makes your service special. And remember this words clearly – 'by their fruits, you shall know them'. Those additional things, extra energy and time, hard work and what have you, that you put in your job are your fruits. And good fruits come from good trees, see it? Clearly, I guess.

So if you want to keep that job of yours if you want to retain that office or get the management to move you up to a better one instead of showing you the door, start being committed. Be dedicated to your job and a befitting reward will eventually come to you.

See You At The Top!